# BASEBALL

## UNDERDOG STORIES

### BY MARTY GITLIN

## UNDERDOG
## SPORTS STORIES

SportsZone

An Imprint of Abdo Publishing | abdobooks.com

**abdobooks.com**

Published by Abdo Publishing, a division of ABDO, PO Box 398166, Minneapolis, Minnesota 55439.
Copyright © 2019 by Abdo Consulting Group, Inc. International copyrights reserved in all countries.
No part of this book may be reproduced in any form without written permission from the publisher.
SportsZone™ is a trademark and logo of Abdo Publishing.

Printed in the United States of America, North Mankato, Minnesota
092018
012019

THIS BOOK CONTAINS
RECYCLED MATERIALS

Cover Photo: Kathy Willens/AP Images
Interior Photos: AP Images, 5, 8, 15, 16, 19, 21, 22; New York Daily News/Getty Images, 6; Leonard
McCombe/The LIFE Images Collection/Getty Images, 11; Walter Iooss Jr./Sports Illustrated/Getty
Images, 13; Herb Scharfman/Sports Illustrated/Getty Images, 25; Robert Beck/Icon Sportswire/AP
Images, 27; Al Behrman/AP Images, 29; John Swart/AP Images, 30–31; Eric Risberg/AP Images, 32; Amy
Sancetta/AP Images, 35, 42, 44–45; Charles Krupa/AP Images, 36–37; Bill Kostroun/AP Images, 39, 41

Editor: Patrick Donnelly
Series Designer: Melissa Martin

**Library of Congress Control Number: 2018949194**

**Publisher's Cataloging-in-Publication Data**

Names: Gitlin, Marty, author.
Title: Baseball underdog stories / by Marty Gitlin.
Description: Minneapolis, Minnesota : Abdo Publishing, 2019 | Series: Underdog sports stories |
        Includes online resources and index.
Identifiers: ISBN 9781532117596 (lib. bdg.) | ISBN 9781532170454 (ebook)
Subjects: LCSH: Baseball--Juvenile literature. | Upsets in sports--Juvenile literature. | Winning and
        losing--Juvenile literature.
Classification: DDC 796.357--dc23

# TABLE OF CONTENTS

# CHAPTER 1

# A GIANT UPSET

Underdogs have always been part of baseball lore. They are the teams that fans love to root for, despite the odds being stacked against them. They are not supposed to win pennants. They are not supposed to win the World Series. But sometimes they find a way. One of those teams was the 1954 New York Giants.

The Cleveland Indians had set an American League (AL) record by winning 111 games that year. They finally halted

The unusual dimensions of the Polo Grounds played a big part in the 1954 World Series.

Willie Mays makes one of the most remarkable catches in baseball history.

the dynasty of the New York Yankees, who had won the

previous five World Series. The Indians boasted one of the

premier pitching staffs in baseball history. And they led the

AL in home runs.

Meanwhile, the Giants appeared destined to be dominated in the World Series. They had peaked in early July. Their record after the All-Star break was a ho-hum 40–30. That was hardly a mark that planted fear in the hearts of the powerful Indians.

As the series began in New York, the experts thought the Indians would sweep the Giants. Their prediction gained strength when Cleveland jumped out to a 2–0 lead in the first inning of Game 1. But the Giants held tough and took a 2–2 tie into the eighth inning. Then, thanks to one of the greatest plays in baseball history and the unusual dimensions of New York's ballpark, the series took a dramatic turn.

The first two Cleveland batters reached base. Then Indians first baseman Vic Wertz slammed a ball to deep center field. It looked like a sure extra-base hit that would drive in two runs. But there was a lot of room in center field at New York's Polo Grounds—483 feet, to be exact. And the Giants' center fielder that day was no ordinary player.

Future Hall of Famer Willie Mays turned at the crack of the bat and sprinted with his back to home plate.

Dusty Rhodes, *center*, is greeted by his Giants teammates at home plate after his game-winning home run in Game 1.

He reached up and caught the ball over his shoulder just to the right of the 483 feet sign. Mays turned and fired it back to the infield as the runners scampered back to their bases. Many people still consider the catch to be the greatest in baseball history. And the Giants escaped the inning without giving up a run.

Pinch-hitter Dusty Rhodes ended the game with one of the most memorable home runs in World Series history. He faced Indians ace Bob Lemon

## DYNAMITE DUSTY

World Series hero Dusty Rhodes played just seven seasons in the major leagues. He never batted more than 244 times in a season. But he sure could hit. He received NL Most Valuable Player (MVP) votes in 1954 after batting .341 with 15 home runs and 50 runs batted in (RBI) in just 164 at-bats.

with two on and one out in the 10th inning. Rhodes hit a pop fly down the right field line that carried just far enough to reach the Polo Grounds' "short porch" 258 feet away from home plate. The stunning home run gave the Giants a 5–2 victory.

New York took the momentum and ran with it. Rhodes hit another home run as the Giants and pitcher Johnny Antonelli won Game 2 at home 3–1. The series shifted to Cleveland, where the National League (NL) champions kept rolling. Rubén Gómez shut down the high-powered Indians while Mays collected three hits and drove in three runs in a 6–2 victory. That left New York one game away from the title.

The Indians tried to put up a fight in Game 4. New York had jumped out to a 7–0 lead before Cleveland rallied for four unanswered runs. But Antonelli came on to pitch in relief of starter Don Liddle, and he shut the door. Antonelli struck out both batters he faced in the eighth inning. He then retired the Indians in the ninth to clinch the World Series for New York.

Giants manager Leo Durocher, *left*, and Rhodes were all smiles as the series shifted to Cleveland for Game 3.

The Giants swept the Indians in four straight. They held Cleveland's hard-hitting offense to just nine runs and a team batting average of .190 in four games.

Already an All-Star, Mays's legend began to grow with his amazing catch. And the mighty Indians could only shake their heads and wonder what might have happened if Wertz had hit that ball in any other park, or with any other player out in center field.

# CHAPTER 2

# RED-HOT RED SOX

The Boston Red Sox of the 1940s and '50s were relatively consistent winners. The team that played its home games at famed Fenway Park usually placed behind the dominant New York Yankees. But they almost always ended the season with a winning record.

The Red Sox had finished with a winning record in 16 of the previous 20 years heading into 1959. Then their bubble burst. They finished below the .500 mark every season

Carl Yastrzemski was locked in at the plate for the Boston Red Sox in 1967

# THE AMAZING YAZ

Carl Yastrzemski had many great seasons during his Hall of Fame career. But it's easy to pick out his best. That was 1967. The man they called "Yaz" won a rare Triple Crown that year when he led the AL with a .326 batting average, 44 home runs, and 121 runs batted in.

from 1959 to 1966. And they were showing no signs of improvement. In 1965 they lost 100 games for the first time in 33 years, and they dropped 90 more in 1966.

It's not like their lineup was terrible. The Red Sox had several solid players. The greatest was future Hall of Famer Carl Yastrzemski. The outfielder had led the AL in doubles three times and won the batting championship in 1963. The Red Sox could hit. But their pitching staff was among the worst in baseball.

Nothing seemed destined to change under new manager Dick Williams in 1967. A terrible stretch early that year dropped the Red Sox into seventh place. Their pitchers allowed an average of seven runs during a nine-game period that dropped the team's record to 14–17. They began to play better in May and June. But the Sox remained seven games out of first place on July 8.

Then, after the All-Star break, the Red Sox suddenly started to win. They took three of four from the Orioles. Then they swept two games from Detroit. They won two

Yastrzemski, *left*, and Twins slugger Harmon Killebrew compare notes before the teams' fateful final series.

Yastrzemski blasts a three-run homer off Twins pitcher Jim Merritt on September 30, 1967.

more in Baltimore. Finally, they went to Cleveland and swept a four-game series with the Indians. The pitching staff performed brilliantly. Veteran right-hander Jim Lonborg emerged as an ace, winning four straight starts.

Yastrzemski smashed six home runs during the streak. The Red Sox won 10 consecutive games to move within a half-game of first place.

The fans began packing Fenway as one of the greatest pennant races in baseball history took shape. Boston, Detroit, Minnesota, and Chicago battled each other for the AL championship the rest of the way. Each team spent at least one day in first place in September.

The race came down to the final weekend. Yastrzemski's three-run homer on Saturday, September 30, helped the Red Sox beat the Twins, leaving the teams tied for first place. The White Sox lost to the Washington Senators and were eliminated. Detroit also lost, falling a game and a half out of first.

That Sunday, the Tigers needed to sweep a doubleheader from the Angels on Sunday to stay alive. If they didn't, the winner of the Twins-Red Sox game at Fenway would clinch the AL pennant.

The fate of the Sox did not look promising early. Minnesota scored twice off Lonborg to forge a 2–0 lead in the third inning. Errors by Yastrzemski and first baseman George Scott cost the Sox two runs.

Meanwhile, Twins standout pitcher Dean Chance was mowing down one hitter after another. Then came the fateful sixth inning. The Red Sox opened the inning with four straight singles. They knocked Chance out of the game. Soon they led 5–2.

That was all Lonborg needed. He rose to the occasion against Twins Rookie of the Year Rod Carew in the ninth inning. With the tying run at the plate and nobody out, Lonborg induced Carew to hit into a double play. One out later and Boston had clinched a tie for the AL pennant. When Detroit dropped the second game of its doubleheader, the Red Sox were headed to the World Series.

The Red Sox swarm pitcher Jim Lonborg after he closed out the Twins and helped Boston win the AL pennant.

The Red Sox nearly completed the Cinderella story. They extended the powerful St. Louis Cardinals to seven games in the World Series before falling. But they had already gained fame as one of the most incredible underdog achievers in baseball history.

# CHAPTER 3

# MIRACLE METS

There is no nice way to say it. When the New York Mets entered the NL in 1962, they were awful. They lost a record 120 games that year, and they followed that up by losing at least 109 games in each of the next three years. Simply put, they were by far the worst team in baseball.

Things had improved a bit heading into 1969. But the Mets were still considered terrible. Nothing they did had

Tom Seaver won 25 games for the surprising Mets in 1969.

changed that view by late May. They were stuck in fourth place with an 18–23 record, nine games out of first place.

Suddenly they came to life. The Mets rattled off 11 straight wins. They gave up just two runs per game during that streak. Budding stars Tom Seaver and Jerry Koosman were leading one of the best pitching staffs in the sport.

Nolan Ryan, *left*, and catcher Jerry Grote celebrate after closing out the Braves in Game 3 of the NLCS.

The Mets had become a strong team. But few believed they could win the NL pennant. After all, they sat 10 games behind the sizzling Chicago Cubs in the league's East Division. And just seven weeks remained in the regular season.

That's when the Mets went from mild to red-hot. Meanwhile, the Cubs collapsed. New York won 12 of 13 in late August. A 10-game winning streak in early September vaulted the Mets into first place. Then they won nine in a row in late September to leave the Cubs and the rest of the NL East in the dust.

## THE STRIKEOUT ARTIST

The most famous player on the 1969 Mets was not very famous at the time. Nolan Ryan was a 22-year-old pitcher in his second year in the majors that season. Ryan would grow into the greatest strikeout pitcher ever. He led his league in strikeouts 11 times and finished his career with an incredible 5,714 strikeouts. That is a record that might never be broken.

Only the Atlanta Braves stood in the way of a World Series berth. The Mets steamrolled past the Braves in three straight games in the National League Championship Series (NLCS). This time it was their hitting that carried them. Outfield standouts Cleon Jones and Tommie Agee led an attack that posted 27 runs in the sweep.

A powerful Baltimore team awaited in the World Series. The Orioles had won 109 games. They boasted tremendous pitching. They hit for power. They played brilliant defense. They were a machine.

But the Mets dismantled that machine. Agee played the role of hero in a 5–0 victory to give the Mets the series lead to stay in Game 3. He smashed a home run leading off the first inning. He tracked down a blast in center field to save two runs in the fourth inning. Agee then made a diving catch with the bases loaded to end the seventh.

The Orioles never recovered. The Mets won four straight after losing the opener. Koosman and Seaver

Tommie Agee makes the play to keep the Orioles off the board in Game 3.

combined to win three games. The Mets held the Orioles to just 23 hits in the entire series. The Birds managed a meager .146 batting average in five games.

Surprise teams had won championships before and they've won championships since. But no bigger underdog in the history of baseball ever wore a World Series crown than the Miracle Mets of 1969.

# CHAPTER 4

# CINDERELLA CINCINNATI

The Cincinnati Reds dominated the NL in the 1970s, winning six division titles, four pennants, and two World Series during the decade. But by 1990, the Big Red Machine was no more than a distant memory.

The Reds lost a team-record 101 games in 1982, and their return to contention was a bumpy process. Every time they took a step forward, it seemed they'd take two steps back the next season. After a 75–87 campaign in

In 1990 few players in baseball were more exciting to watch than Reds outfielder Eric Davis.

1989, few expected much from the team at the start of a new decade.

But appearances can be deceiving. The 1990 Reds used a balanced offensive attack and a sensational bullpen to win the NL West. Shortstop Barry Larkin and third baseman Chris Sabo had All-Star seasons. Outfielder Eric Davis was a dynamic star. But no Reds player hit more than 25 home runs or drove in more than 86 runs.

The Reds were also lucky. They played in a weak division. They remained in first place from the first day of the season to the last. Then they defeated the Pittsburgh Pirates in six games to advance to the World Series.

That is when the success was expected to end. The mighty Oakland Athletics were the defending world champions and had won three straight AL pennants. They featured the incredible 1–2 power punch of Jose Canseco and Mark McGwire, a.k.a. "the Bash Brothers." McGwire slammed 39 home runs that year and Canseco

Oakland's Bash Brothers—Mark McGwire and Jose Canseco—
were the stars of the Athletics' intimidating lineup.

hit 37. They also had power and speed in the leadoff spot

with Rickey Henderson, the most prolific base stealer in

baseball history.

And their pitching was even more dominant. The

Athletics had the lowest team earned run average (ERA) in

the league. Bob Welch and Dave Stewart combined for an

incredible 49 victories, while ace closer Dennis Eckersley saved 48 games.

Few expected the Reds to be able to compete against powerful Oakland. Many experts believed the World Series would end in a sweep. And they were right—sort of. Cincinnati shocked the world by winning four straight games to complete its fairy-tale season.

An unlikely hero emerged in the stunning series. Journeyman outfielder Billy Hatcher was playing for his fourth team in seven seasons. He worked his way into the starting lineup but wasn't a big contributor. Then in Game 1, Hatcher had three hits and scored three runs in a

Billy Hatcher got hot at the right time for Cincinnati.

7–0 victory. Davis hit a two-run homer off Stewart in the first inning, and Reds ace Jose Rijo tossed seven shutout innings to stifle the Athletics batters.

Game 2 proved far more tense. Trailing 4–3 in the eighth, Hatcher led off with a triple, his fourth hit of the game. He scored on a groundout to tie the game. Then in the 10th inning the Reds ripped three straight singles off Eckersley to win it 5–4 and take a 2–0 series lead.

The World Series shifted to Oakland, where the Reds continued to roll. A seven-run third inning keyed an 8–3 victory in Game 3. Hatcher finally cooled off—he *only*

## THE NASTY BOYS

The trio that carried the Cincinnati bullpen in 1990 had a colorful nickname. The hard-throwing threesome were known as "the Nasty Boys." Lefties Randy Myers and Norm Charlton and right-hander Rob Dibble combined to strike out 351 batters in 339 innings and the Reds led the NL with 50 saves that season.

had two hits—but Sabo hit a pair of home runs, Tom Browning threw six strong innings, and the bullpen took care of the rest.

Rickey Henderson exemplifies the frustrations of Oakland hitters after striking out against Jose Rijo in Game 4.

Rijo finished the job with a masterpiece in Game 4. He allowed one run on two hits and struck out nine batters. The Reds overcame a 1–0 deficit with two runs in the eighth inning, and Randy Myers got the final two outs to finish the sweep.

Few teams in history have entered a World Series as a bigger underdog than the 1990 Cincinnati Reds. That they beat powerful Oakland was surprising. That they swept the Athletics was shocking.

# CHAPTER 5

# REVERSING THE CURSE

It was known as "the Curse of the Bambino." Boston Red Sox fans knew the story by heart. The Curse accounted for every blunder, fluke, and mishap on and off the field that had prevented their beloved team from winning a World Series since 1918. And most of them involved the hated New York Yankees.

The Curse traced back to when the Sox sold Babe Ruth—sometimes called "the Bambino"—to the Yankees

David Ortiz came up with big hit after big hit as the Red Sox rallied against the Yankees.

before the 1920 season. The list of unbelievable defeats that followed would take an entire New England winter to recite. The years became a kind of shorthand in conversation between Red Sox fans. 1946. 1975. 1978. 1986. 1999. 2003. Each defeat featured a unique form of agonizing frustration.

Millions of Boston fans had been born, lived full lives, and died since the team's most recent World Series championship. It was growing more maddening by the year. And when the Red Sox lost the first three games of the 2004 ALCS to—who else?— the Yankees, it seemed like a lost cause. After all, the Yankees had pounded

Mark Bellhorn emerged as an unlikely hero in the ALCS.

the Red Sox 19–8 in Game 3. And no team had ever lost the first three games and come back to win a series in baseball history.

A sweep seemed likely when the Yankees took a 4–3 lead heading into the ninth inning of Game 4. The Sox faced the tall task of beating Mariano Rivera, the greatest closer in baseball history. Boston was three outs from elimination. But Kevin Millar walked, pinch runner Dave Roberts stole second base, and Bill Mueller drove him in with a single to send it into extra innings.

## THE STORY OF BIG PAPI

David Ortiz was not just one of the greatest designated hitters in baseball history. He was also one of its most beloved players ever. His clutch hitting was legendary. Ortiz seemed to get better as he got older. In 2016 he led the American League with 127 runs batted in at age 40.

Red Sox slugger David Ortiz won it with a home run in the 12th inning. The momentum had shifted. But Boston still had to win three more games in a row. The Sox kept grinding. Trailing 4–2 in the eighth inning of Game 5, Ortiz homered and Roberts again scored the tying run after pinch running for Millar. Ortiz singled in the winning run in the 14th inning. Back in New York for Game 6, a three-run homer by Mark Bellhorn and seven sparkling innings from Curt Schilling set up a showdown for the pennant.

Boston had become a steamroller. Ortiz hit a two-run homer in the first inning of Game 7. Outfielder Johnny Damon blasted a grand slam in the second. He hit another home run, as did Bellhorn. The Red Sox completed one of the most amazing comebacks ever with a 10–3 rout.

The Red Sox were unstoppable. They made it eight straight wins with a four-game sweep of the St. Louis Cardinals in the World Series for their first championship in

Johnny Damon, *left*, watches the ball after hitting a grand slam off Yankees pitcher Javier Vazquez in Game 7.

86 years. They allowed just three runs to the Cardinals over the last three games.

That event was a bit anticlimactic. It was the incredible comeback against the Yankees that earned its place in history as an ultimate underdog achievement.

# CHAPTER 6

# CARDINALS FLY HIGH

H all of Fame pitcher Lefty Gomez once said it's better to be lucky than good. That can certainly be true for sports teams. The 2006 St. Louis Cardinals were a prime example.

The Redbirds finished the regular season with a mediocre mark of 83–78. But they were fortunate that the NL Central Division provided little competition. Their record was strong enough to win it.

Yadier Molina celebrates as he rounds the bases after hitting a go-ahead home run in Game 7 of the NLCS.

David Eckstein's double in the eighth inning of Game 4 against the Tigers was the key hit in the series for St. Louis.

The Cardinals did not hit the ball particularly well. Despite the greatness of slugger Albert Pujols, they placed just sixth in the league in runs scored. They did not feature a great pitching staff. Among their starting pitchers, only

Chris Carpenter posted an ERA under 4.00 and the team placed ninth in the NL in that category. St. Louis was even only a bit above average in fielding.

Nobody anticipated much when the playoffs began. But the Cardinals proved that they were both lucky *and* good. They also proved an old saying in baseball: Good pitching beats good hitting.

Their pitching staff was locked in during the postseason. The Cardinals allowed just six runs in four games to defeat San Diego in the NL Division Series. Then they surrendered four runs or fewer in five of seven games against the heavily favored

## AMAZING ALBERT

Albert Pujols enjoyed perhaps his finest season in 2006 with a career-high 49 home runs. But it's hard to pick his best year. After all, he scored and drove in at least 99 runs every season from 2001 to 2011. It's no wonder that he won three NL Most Valuable Player awards along the way.

New York Mets in the NLCS. Catcher Yadier Molina hit a tie-breaking home run in the ninth inning of Game 7. Then rookie Adam Wainwright slammed the door in the bottom half of the inning to send the Cardinals to the World Series.

That set up a World Series showdown against the Detroit Tigers. With the top pitching staff in the AL and a balanced batting attack that blasted 203 home runs in the regular season, the Tigers were a formidable foe.

But they were no match for St. Louis. The Cardinals' starting trio of Carpenter, Anthony Reyes, and Jeff Weaver helped limit Detroit to just 10 earned runs in five games. The hitting heroes were third baseman Scott Rolen and 5-foot-6 shortstop David Eckstein, who each collected a series-high eight hits.

The critical moment came in Game 4 after the Cardinals had won two of the first three. The Tigers clawed ahead 3–0 in the third. The Cardinals chipped away and took a 4–3 lead in the seventh, but Detroit tied it at 4–4 in the eighth inning. Then Eckstein played the hero. His two-out double in the bottom of the eighth drove in the go-ahead run. Wainwright retired the Tigers 1–2–3 in the ninth and St. Louis was one win away from the title.

The Cardinals never lost the momentum. They became world champions with a 4–2 victory in Game 5. And in doing so, they proved that the best team does not always win the title. It's often the team that gets hot at the right time.

The Cardinals celebrate after Adam Wainwright (50) slammed the door on Detroit to clinch the World Series.

# GLOSSARY

**bullpen**

The area on a baseball field where relief pitchers can warm up; also a way to refer to a team's relief pitchers as a group.

**closer**

A pitcher who comes in at the end of the game to secure a win for his team.

**contention**

Involvement in a race for a championship.

**dynasty**

A team that has an extended period of success, usually winning multiple championships in the process.

**error**

A mistake in the field made by a baseball player.

**favored**

Considered likely to win.

**pennant**

An American League or National League championship.

**prolific**

Very productive.

**underdog**

The person or team that is not expected to win.

# MORE INFORMATION

## BOOKS

Berman, Len. *The Greatest Moments in Sports: Upsets and Underdogs*. Naperville, IL: Sourcebooks Jabberwocky, 2012.

Editors of Sports Illustrated Kids. *Sports Illustrated Kids Big Book of WHO Baseball*. New York: Time, 2017.

Jacobs, Greg. *The Everything Kids' Baseball Book: From Baseball's History to Today's Favorite Players—With Lots of Home Run Fun in Between*. Avon, MA: Adams Media, 2014.

# ONLINE RESOURCES

**Booklinks**
NONFICTION NETWORK
FREE! ONLINE NONFICTION RESOURCES

To learn more about baseball underdogs, visit abdobooklinks.com. These links are routinely monitored and updated to provide the most current information available.

# INDEX

# ABOUT THE AUTHOR

Marty Gitlin is a freelance educational book author based in Cleveland, Ohio. He has had more than 140 books published, many in the realm of sports. He also won more than 45 awards as a newspaper sportswriter from 1991 to 2002. Included was a first place for general excellence from Associated Press in 1996. That organization also selected him as one of the top four feature writers in Ohio.